TIME AND THE TREE

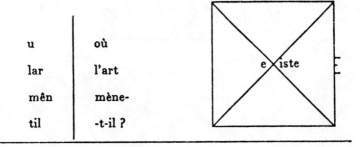

u	où
lar	l'art
mên	mène-
til	-t-il ?

car le Silence

eXiste

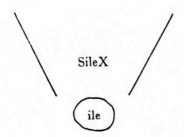

SileX

Roger Giroux

TIME AND THE TREE

Translated by Anthony Barnett

Open Township

Published in 1987 by Open Township, 14 Foster Clough, Heights Road, Hebden Bridge, W. Yorks., in an edition of 333 copies, of which this is number 9.

Designed & typeset by Open Township; printed by the Arc & Throstle Press, Todmorden, Lancs.

ISBN 0 948757 02 7

A bibliography of works by Roger Giroux (1925-1974) is included in the posthumously published *L'autre temps* Ed. Unes 1984.

The frontispiece reproduces a page of "Est-ce", Roger Giroux's last text, published in *Argile* XIX—XX, Maeght Editeur 1979. It shows why "silex" (Eng.) is preferred to "flint" as a translation of "silex" (Fr.) in the penultimate poem of the section of *Time and the Tree* entitled "The Almond".

The cover shows a nineteenth century Japanese woodblock print designed for fabric, courtesy of the translator.

TRANSLATOR'S NOTE

I began this translation in the late 1970s. I found a practice, not rationalized in every poem individually, allowing certain philological resolutions for the whole. I have benefited from conversations with different persons, and from reading critically, the occasional appearance of a few of the poems in other translations. The publication in 1982 of the author's 'Lettre à Anthony Rudolf' was most useful. My publishers have persuaded me, rightly, I think, of the inappropriateness of 'Arbor Hour', and similarly imaginative exercises in translating the title; and they have been most gracious in their acceptance of late amendments. I wish to express my thanks to Mme Damienne Giroux, and to Mercure de France, publishers of the French text, for their kind permission in allowing the publication of this edition; and to Paul Auster, editor of the *Random House Book of Twentieth-Century French Poetry* (New York, 1982); corrected edition (New York 1984), where eight of these translations, some in earlier drafts, were first printed.

A.B.

FINDING WORDS AGAIN

I was the object of a question of no real concern to me. It was, simply, there, calling me by name, softly, so as not to frighten me. But I had nothing with which to keep track of the sound of its voice. So I named it absence, and I imagined my mouth (or my hands) was about to bleed. My hands stayed spotless. My mouth was a round pebble on a dune of fine sand: no wind, only the smell of the sea mingling with the pines.

I wanted then to describe a landscape: it haunted me. And I haunted this landscape where a tree was standing. The tree held out its arms blindly to possess the land-scape, and I took up precisely that part of space where the tree was going to send out its word over the land-scape.

What rose from the heart of the tree, I had no way of saying:

For out of this landscape no voice broke, no face. Too many signs remained ambiguous: I saw a great eagle, a whole moon, and the sea, at noon, under the future palms. I lived in a garden, the shadow of a poem. April was a rare bird. I was verging on a lie. (The tree waited to be named.)

I have no other home than this sentence without context, half round. Every word drowns in a ridiculous perfume.

I have no other home than this absent face. . .

A silence in the past, that was the site of this absence: a pure space, a point.

What sentence could ever express this movement without a home, this pure power: *suffering not suffering?*

4

No swallows, no willow. But, in the beginning, the tera-toid blindness of the poem.

And I say the calm face of the water in a mountain trough: a traveller comes here to wash, from what soli-tude? He sinks, to the depths of its silence. And the snow-covered scene holds the secret of winter. Then the stinging of a star.

In this ageless and unwonted land, too clear, the voice freezes.

And I live in a silent expectation. Detached, only by the length of a name, this is my place, this one word, gaping.

5

Life, so close. A man goes by. He is singing. The sounds of evening. The shadow and its hues. A tree (or is it a soul watching?) The sky, geometric.

But no sentence is given.

This act of writing exerting me, is it the flesh bleeding, with an unspeakable world? These wounded words, I suffer because of the wound (and I do not suffer.) Every mouth tells a lie, if it is not a kiss.

Sentences! Don't you want me to live? Who would be able to say blood is here, breath is this?

Who would dare. . . ?

On gaining possession of his shadows, the poet occupies a disproportionate space: transparency. Is this a tragedy, or the bird singing at the centre of the cross? Given at least the height of breath, is there any word for him other than the mean?

At the crossroad of blood and light, the sentence would become pure gold.

Dust of being, profusion of perceptible words, foliage moving in the water of the soul, pulsation of many minutes. . . and I am left speechless in the finespun prison of the senses.

To be this, multiple, at the point of trembling, shivering and trembling in the interval of blood and light, at the birth of love.

Nothing is ever said. And, always, saying this nothing. Perpetual birth of the poet. And is he going to tear off his face? For it is there he says he can see, before all space. And who will triumph, a scream stifling him, or the joy, he cannot communicate?

No fable.

From one silence to the next, in the same question, the poem falters.

He *is breathing. His words fall on the trees, the houses: mouth to mouth, the blossom*. . . (through a vale runs a stream.)

This is his nostalgia: man.

The wooded, winding line of a hill. Three houses, home in the evening. The space of a stream bordered by gardens. Then the sky, almost white.

And this is my exile: this page imprinted with the steps of a slumbering giant.

It swarms in the opaque, anthers at the point of Transparency, and touches on the feminine place of the poem.

Shuttling of the sentence: *the pupil protrudes.*

There is a point in the soul, a place without breadth where silence and speech become one and descend on the spirit, flooding it, and drowning it: this is the moment when the eye at the centre of the Voice opens.

At the edge of the ORCHARD, the archer was lying down: he was still breathing, and it was LIKE an imprisoned star, for there, in a tiny little point, was a fantastic space where there was a star, and for all that it was not there. But it was LIKE a wall of silence going to vanish, and it was LIKE a door never going to be closed again. It was LIKE an eye going to open, and LIKE a mouth going to speak. And when the archer would no longer have any breath, then there would be a mouth, and another mouth to know it. And henceforth this fantastic space would have a name, and the sky be able to breathe again, over there, right at the end of the ORCHARD.

PINE

I sing a tree. The trunk stands bare up to a clump of foliage the breeze hardly stirs, arranging itself around numerous rents. It is nothing but holes, frills and ruffs. Yet this pine proceeds from a strict order whose tortuous appearance betrays austerity. If it lives in a landscape inclined by everything towards composure, it is the better to disguise its inner bearing. For it belongs nowhere. It is a place unto itself. It is alone.

Birds haunt its disquieting presence unwillingly: a crow, sometimes, rests there, but never stays. Even the stars only pass by the holes in this tatter, for fear of a single cicada's derision. And I know of no skies more songful than the sky skirting its crown: its ears thin out to transparency, its fingers respond to caresses from afar. . . A ballet is being staged, in which it is shepherd, magus, messenger. You cannot tell any longer, by the light or the smell, if this is vertigo.

And I find I have come a little further at these sentences exit. Where is the pine? And why would it need my voice to sing? Not enough its night wood, its leaf chemistry? If I were not there. . .

11

Pine hidden in the pine, pine hidden in the tree. The tree howls in the tree, and the tree prays in the tree, and this is its only word: to be a tree! What is a tree? What is this escaping, again and again, in a delirium of forests, ships, poems?

If I were not there. . .

Pine cones for lighting the fire in winter. . .

DESCRIBING THE LANDSCAPE

Autumn has come,
As if I did not exist.
And I do not know if it remembers. . .

And my word has only the space
Of this imaginary line
Where my face imprisons it.

And however far I lean over the waters of the poem,
I see only a bird, flying away from me
Towards a vision of winter.

I am living in an empty landscape
In the legend of summer.

And the snow, motionless, leans
Over my lips, becoming white.

It questions this absence
Coming out of it.

It forgets even the sky.

And perhaps words are pure appearances
Between the sky and my face. . .

Snow is falling,
Out of the spectrum.
And now my eyes dare not breathe.

My soul loses all consciousness,
And the measure of this land.

And I am no longer one.

Silent blinded face. . .

What light would not shatter
Its glaze against the lips!

O the idea of the wellspring, a song
Denying itself there,

                  this beauty
Forever faded. . .

The colour of the sea is like morning.
The sky is filled with birds the wind has left.
There are vessels, ships and boats.
And fruit, serene,
Waits for summer to bring it light.

And we pass, through the invisible lock.
And in the wide blue valleys of the heart
Where memory does not reach
A sail draws near, between appearances,
Signalling to silence the name of the landscape.

And the trees retreat in autumn
Covering our steps in their dying waves.
A shadow moves, among the hills,
And then, what is left of this land, but some snow
Falling, in the palm of the hand?

The impossible silence fulfills its space,
And here, slowly, my image destroys.
My eyes forget,
And my face dies, mirrored, absent,
Like a dream, at the edge of a branch, in its flower.

A bird, as it flies, out to sea,
Carrying the memory of land to the end of this day
Of light and love, a bird. . .

How say this and not undo the work
Of eyes, hands, and every part of the face,
And not snap in us bird and language. . .
How say this and not blush, in silence?

Every work is closed, every word absent,
And the poem laughs and defies me to live
This longing for a space where no time would be.
And this is a gift of the blue, this power to name

A bird, as it flies, out to sea, like a breath,
This moment lasting only to die, out there,
From world beginning to the last wreck,
And perhaps even further, towards the last star,
The first word, O how say this. . .

(Talking to trees becomes a calm man, when he doubts, in the end, the gift of prophecy. Let a bat rest under his hand: he looks at it. Then he listens. He is master of all that leans. Sometimes, a tree falls...

He no longer proceeds from night, pride, or dream: he precedes the hours. He secretes an invisible space, overhung by a rose of flesh, O wondrous innocence of the void!

The calm man, often, works, on a table of white wood, on writings at rest, while, over there, others hold life as a precious thing, a useful wisdom! And the calm man, out of sight, on a delible page, discovers over there, on the other side, a plain man at work, knowing nothing about him.)

WHERE I AM

What should I build with my tongue?
What palace mad with despair
Haunted by immovable absences?
What city, destined, then as now
To the pure silences of oblivion?

Arbor, ardour, solitude, dust. . .

And it is as if I did not exist
In this immensity separating me from myself,
In what is untouchable here
Teratoid, trembling. . .

What is it? What is this
Touching me, and leaving me?
What serenity freezes me?
What cry of being here!
What silence in the heart's grey waste!
What immobility!
What invisible night!

The centre is black,
And speech does not assuage the leprous face.
Its power flags, outside the circle,
And grounds, at the edge of a cold star.

And it is night, the faint fall.
And the sky turns in the hand in drawing away
From the heart.

(In calling what face? Imagining what love?
The saying of the poem is powerless?
It obliterates life giving words,
And prolongs the death of an unappeased dawn?)

What soul in its grave has pronounced this?
What mouth trembling with cold
Amid the devastated space of light?

O mortal agony is a heady flower!
And the occasional passer-by,
Archaeologist, shepherd or maiden,
Would search in vain for sign of Memory
Once oracle over the City. . .

This sentence, doubting (this innocent
sentence, imperceptibly silenced), beautiful image
uncertain of living, O transparent grief,
O mirror, this sentence (implausible)
longing for me, looks for my face,
and stops me, blinding me, in the middle of the road. . .

No doubt it is dying, this impotent sentence
doubting, tempting me, and with only the memory
of this doubt where I am. . .
                              I cannot say,

and I listen to the sky. I watch the water.
And the sound of my voice awakes only the echo
of an immovable absence, a surfeit of silence
in the night of a sentence knowing nothing. . .

Far from everything, far from myself, I enter my life.
I doubt whether love will remember being here.
I doubt my eyes, my name, my shadow.
I doubt death,
                    silence,
                              doubt. . .

What place is this without words for me,
With nothing for me to say
Except my presentiment of a pit
Where the heart should be, avoiding me?

And what voice is this, speaking, deep inside me,
In the slumber and warmth of a louder
And deeper voice speaking
And unheard by me?

Who but my voice can say if I live,
If I dream, or doubt with it?
Speaking is not living,
And living outside my voice is my death twice.

                    If I die,
Who will know, but this voice
Speaking, and not hearing me?

(Loftier than mirror, it tries the death
Drawing back before it, with shadows
And silence, lasting only
A soul, a movement of the lips. . .)

27

Violated Face,
O light, Black Virgin
stifled in flight!

And being here in the cold
of the poem, astonishes me.

And I cannot die elsewhere.

(Once more time withdraws,
releasing me from the memory
of wide solitary margins
and leaving me where it is pure
in a foreclosed garden
covert of fern and ruin
where I am, living, gazed at
(in a non space)
from the depths of inanimate air,
irrespirable, noxious. . .)

THE ALMOND

A lake is here, blue. A sail
Free of all thought, on the sky
And on the water (a sail)
So doubly beautiful (free
of all thought) the sight
(this sail) forgets anew
And loosens under the lap
(here, calm) bobbing about, the algae
of desire downed. . .

And no longer feels anything but this: beautiful, bare,
The better to wed the blank whiteness
To its head long held down. . .

Sail!
Absent sail I see
Encroaching on the distance. . .

Absent:
This voice speaks of a shore dazzled by time,
And no longer distinguishes from the soul at sleep
The oh so sweet, impure, gestures of death.

Speaking,
And dreaming only of moon
Tree, waves, seasons.
Speaking, and fading, improbably,
In the incurable dawn, the sands,
The wind.

(Queen of going, long ago
And, closer than all,
Being herself desire,
She said I shall come,
Like placing flowers
In a sudden shaft of light:

This room where I am,
One perfect morning. . .)

She is saying: this shadow, this perfume,
This death unfolding. . .
I am speaking and I exist.

There, in her oversized sepulchre of chalk,
Me, everyone I have asked here
In the hope, perhaps. . .

There. The gentle slope of her face.
Me, brittle imprint of a mouth, at the edges.

Like the shadows in the room
(as from the height of pretence
too clear a vision of the dark
pales the abyss) she watches:
An unspeakable absence of things.

High up. On the branch where the mask
Eyes, and stills in its cry
A body Everlasting.

What dawn was the flower, the last soul
from where you will appear
out of me, every sail
turned to light behind this time,
would my face draw back
and deny all memory of unnamed shores
listening to their dying at your mirror's edge

far from the consequences?

Naked,
Coming in a shiver,
Becoming herself without reason, not knowing
What pretence at love to be calling in image
(beautiful as unrealized doubt
wave after wave,
unable to come to the lips), here
from one who is no more
than the name of her sham substance

Mirror, unseemly skiff,
water of pure silex.

If life is not this, save this thought
I must keep to myself, unsettling,
Loveliest fruit of a flown angel,

Let fall, from tree to tree,
And even as I remember
(and grant this night
of four feet of windswept umbel,
a last time,
the space of an empty face
like a path, the sea)
This star, this cry, upon the sea:

If life is not this, whether the sands
And silences of this time.

LEGACY

I

The wellspring is the path.
Desire is the wellspring.

And desire is stilled
In the middle of the path.

II

Silence is the wellspring.
Speech is the path.

Speech is the wellspring
And silence of the path.

HOME

Absent home:
A dazzling memory comes to the lips
Amid the purple
And desert of this mouth
Come to drink, felucca
At its eternity.

Lost beauty does not despair
Of a forbidden word.
Out of an angel kept silent
A sail is set
Upon the sea.

And, behind each gate
repeated indefinately over the snow
(soft as a fieldfare crossing the whole expanse)
the same scene of a hanging.

(It emanates from here as an acquiescence,
A new absence, enamoured of light
Surviving love, and squandered by a
Gesture far out in this time.)

Surface of no sound: seabird, birch,
Cupidity in the sky and, higher still,
Between trees and music,
Great blue lakes of uncertainty.

It was before spoken things.
Knowing the star and the moment.
The naked lamp in its kingdom.

She has doubts, and fears the depths of privation:
Her miracle, wounded. Elusive,
Like crossing the shadow of a white poplar.

To desire, she lets silence,
A foam fire for the heart, naked islands
At the whim of winter's silky murmur.

Come so far, true to her divided
Word.

She is living on whiteness
In the blue of oblivion
And the most humble parenthesis
Offered
To the poem, still. . .

Pledged to other precipices.

(Her memory moves among the days.

Unveiled, like an old book of secrets
In the naked wind of things, abandoned soul
Known without an echo.
                    Known,
Not knowing what image has held her image
Captive, at the feet of a star.)

She says who can be, she
Absent who dies, gazing at dying.

Tearfully absent:
And the sign would be the night of the night
(and when time shatters)
Inviting home a similar answer
And losing her gaze.

POEMS

impalpable murder of an object

and the ultimate knowledge
of existing

holding the air
the space of an abandoned
                              boat

night passes through the heart

the host retires to a cloud

some part of an island is held
in suspense
                    like a tree

is it time
                    if it is snowing
with an unforgettable sleep?

far
    like a thread

as if part of me were leaving
river amid the river
rose no rose
perfects

elsewhere
        delicate skin
        when night falls

        almost an end
        on a bed of transparent sand

still harp
a path floats in breathing in
                              fire

is this the purest image?

                              is the soul
where souls of oblivion go
gift of an imaginary absent?

sails
hopelessly innocent of prodigy

touched with the lips
the passage of the light
the white thorn on the pane
still this
      without this

          without a sound

we shall never know
what shadow

         the invisible
distance of the self

its throes before the body

it seems
when the time comes
if need be
high up
under the lamp

foam

flakes off the wall
this indifferent
star

eagle
in memory

in seeing.